Maiden

Mother

Crone

Maiden

Mother

Crone

poems

Madeleine F White

Sea Crow Press

BY MADELEINE F WHITE

Mother of Floods

The Horse and the Girl

CONTENTS

Maiden

Mother

Crone

PREFACE
MOTHER MAIDEN CRONE

Maiden, Mother, Crone
Maiden, Mother, Crone
Moon waxing and waning, I'm never alone.
The faster I go, the faster it follows –
I turn to face my tomorrows.

I am. Pain tells me I am.
Knowledge of how my body fits where it shouldn't,
already some bits floating
in the bath where flesh flashes;
A gurgling laugh. Thumb in mouth. Plugged.
I am.

Child's plumped flesh, pleasant, present.
Thumb in mouth. Plugged.
Silver-fished jumping to winged-hope imaginings
moving beyond the drowning.
Floating silence caught in a radiator's hum.
Gurgled murmurings cut through water-logged memories.
Desire thrums.

Another place. Stuffing of face...
Sick-making, all-eating sweet.
Flesh waxing, spirit waning till thumb unplugged
the Maiden rises and despite surfeit of flesh,
as a fleet-footed deer she evades the spears of unmaking.
The world turns.
Surprise!

Maiden, Mother, Crone
Maiden, Mother, Crone
Moon waxing and waning, I'm never alone.
The faster I go, the faster it follows –
I turn to face my tomorrows.

I am. Pain tells me I am.
She-wolf now I rest a while, but not long.
Plastering my red-painted lupine smile across moon-soaked
streets
I hope the disguise will allow me to pad past silently.
But memories shriek, until I roar.
Claim my place as Mother, not meat.
My cubs will eat.

I demand the earth swallows the shadows that follow.
I will not lie on my back for a tickle.
I am become Bitch, but not for long.
Canine breath exhaling, breathes life into the serpent
I'd curled round my soul to keep their world whole.
A Mother's fangs break the skin.
Upwards and in.

Winding, binding, reminding, finding – I am.
Consuming, colluding, creating – I can.
Breathing fire where there was none
I'm released from the safe-dark
Pain ceases.
I come.

Maiden, Mother, Crone
Maiden, Mother, Crone
Moon waxing and waning, I'm never alone.
The faster I go, the faster it follows –
I turn to face my tomorrows.

I am. Anger has consumed.
An inferno of flame banishes pain.
'Be still my daughter.' No longer lamb to the slaughter.
Mutton now. But mutton is tough.
It must be boiled enough to render it digestible.
I remain indigestible
preferring flame to water.

The same words, the same promises
Serpent-encased-self dragoning
into a world unmade and remade.
Breaking the consistency of constancy with
the power of stillness, entropy's womb.

My womb has shrivelled as I have grown –
Blood's call dripping from incisors bleached by time,
beckoning me from charnel houses and ossuaries.
Path strewn by bones from those like me.

Flesh fails, spirit quails and yet I walk.
Beware. These grey hairs you see are snakes.
They will turn you to stone.
I am Crone.

Maiden, Mother, Crone
Maiden, Mother, Crone
Moon waxing and waning,
I am called home.

PART ONE
MAIDEN

I

The Summoning

Come, come
I am here, hear me.
Come, come
I am here, don't fear me.
Your legs will take you if you let them
and, if you wish your eyes will see.
Come to me.

Chitin carapaces crunching, announce your passing.
Can you feel the rustling under your feet?
You are rightly wary of the creamy nodes that poke
from the web I've spun underground.
Your spirit understands earthbound, you don't yet
so attempt to flee the fairy net.

Steady! Mind that root.
It's in cahoots with the rotting branch lancing itself at you.
Don't fall. Hear! I call more loudly now.
Do you see how I weave? I'm so near.
My web a spider's kiss between branches.
Follow the exhaled silver filigree,
you'll be free while you rest in me.
I promise.

Don't you wish to be held, unspelled by the present?
Crafting carefully, I'll change things into imaginings
softly, softly
Mycelial threads cocooning what must hide, abide inside,
deep, deep.
Yes, sleep, my child, I'll keep your dreams
till you're ready to become what is necessary.

And, as your soul rises, forget.
Run wild without regret, swinging between canopied boughs,
singing songs I've allowed you to keep in this sleep.
Twigs snap and branches break, falling on forest loam.
Beast and tendrils, fruit life spirit, spelling home.

With your passing you wreak brokenness, delicate-leafed tracery
shining it's muted green-veiled response
while forgiving the destruction you are living.
Knowing you are unwoken,
yet that part of you is held.
For now, you crave the freedom of my treedom,
watching the dappling shadows remould and remake themselves
in the wake of your passing.
My crafting holds.

Chaos shapes round what is broken
Knitting and reknitting, becoming.
Did you know, even damaged saplings grow to the light?
They can't help themselves. Maybe you will one day, too.
I'll let go, then, I promise you.

And, flight finally arrested,
floating, you'll twist and turn,
dancing on caressing currents of air
to await the making whole.
Returned.

In order to live a seed must die. I'll spin to connect
as your shoots reach for the sky –
redressing what was, shaping what is become.
I'll breathe, "Fly!"

Conjoined, rejoined
strong enough to
know the unknowable
acknowledge the unthinkable
see the unseeable
bear the unbearable.

In the meantime, though...

Come, come,
I am here, hear me.
Come, come,
I am here, don't fear me.
I'll hold what needs to be hidden in me
Until you can be.

II
Teeth

"Did you do it, did you bite?"

"I did bite."

"Mrs Knight, I'm so sorry,
I can't believe she'd do such a thing.
So sweet-looking, neat-looking, don't you agree?
Though slightly wilder recently... admittedly."

"These phases never last. Don't upset yourself.
But no, it most definitely wasn't anyone else."

"I don't understand why, but she's changed."

"Well, counselling can be arranged. Are there any other
worries?"

"She's in her own world half the time. Not with us,
unless she's making a fuss her thumb's plugged in. Quiet, apart
from.
Apart from now, of course, when she's taken it out. To bite."

"I did bite."

"See she's nodding now, pleased with herself.
ARE YOU SORRY?"

"You'll make yourself hoarse shouting like that. Keep your voice
down Mrs B!"

"Of course. Just upset."

"You'll go on the mat, Mummy!"

"That bite's given us enough of a fright for one day."

"I'm sorry Mrs Knight, I do apologise. I'm starting to doubt my parenting.
This is the last straw in a string of things, I feel quite wrung out."

"I did bite."

"Yes, we know you did. I'm trying to tell your Mummy what happened. How six-year-old Sophie, said three-year old babies needed baby books. Pulled your ones you away from you.
You screamed till you were blue, then bit."

"I did bite."

"Well despite your admission and Sophie's lack of permission for taking your books.
I know she just wanted a look, but still. If you say sorry, yes, just so, I'll let it go."

"Mrs Knight, it's a Kindergarten, and I beg your pardon for this, but isn't it remiss of you not to have kept a closer eye on these two –
and other children in your care. I hear there's even been pulling of hair!"

"Well absolutely Mrs B. If it were up to me there'd be much closer supervision.
The old ways in the good old days were so much better, there was real discipline."

She sniffed to denote her derision.
"All this playing, conveying of ideas, creating with their peers..."
And peered down with a frown.
"Are you sorry at least? Nice girls don't bite."

Bright face wreathed with smiles, the child paused for a while, then thumb unplugged with a plop.

"I did bite, but I did stop."

III
The Faun In The Wardrobe

I looked for a faun in the wardrobe
and the witch and the lion too
it was Nana's in 70s London and I thought that's what we
children should do.

Nearly-nine-year-old me tried the wardrobe,
pulling at the deeply-notched door
wondering aloud to my sister whether anyone'd been in before.

We pitched into pink-blanketed mothballs
the keyhole shining a light,
on what I hoped was a lamppost emerging, through a
breath-fogged crystalline night.

I said to close our eyes tightly,
hold onto the tale that was there –
even though we couldn't quite see it, nor yet feel the bite of
cold air.

With quavering words sliced through darkness
I turned the moonbeam into a knife,
sculpting a powerful spell song to bring deep wild magic to life.

The landscape was one I'd been seeking
in the pages of stories I'd read
wanting the gnawing knowledge confirmed, that's where I
should be instead.

But then, my six-year-old sister called out plaintively –
tremulous voice asking politely, did magic work better on TV?

I tried lingering. Long enough, I thought, to force story-wrapped
letters into words and worlds.
But it wasn't enough. Not enough.

I continued to scour the leaves of books for the wolf-wedded
spider-silked wilderness me,
the one I'd nearly found in a wardrobe.
But the more I looked, the more elusive she became –
reclusive I became.

So where was the popular, slim she who would win things,
be in things, have fun?
Not just the girl whose clothes were too tight,
who couldn't sleep at night.

I heard, "Come."

IV
Changeling

The smoothness of the piano keys feeds her need to please.
But the threads of the Für Elise remain unfurled,
truth unheard.

Instead, she's impaled on practice scales,
their regimented rhythms a mere token
of notes unspoken.

Hostage to hidden-song winter-dream imaginings
her leitmotif stays fixed in the safedark, a missing part –
but as the lark rises so must she. Eventually.

Willing Spring sap into her fingers,
she demands obeisance even as her body's obedience to will
eludes her still.
Flesh uncontained surges beyond winter layers.

Emptying surfeit self onto the keyboard,
her stabbed staccato notes seek to force what is bursting
back into the shell that is hurting.

But skin can't contain pity or pain.
Her lack, the shadow on her back, sought in the passing faces
she scours for signs of her worth.

What if she spoke? Not in music but words.
She knows she'd choke. They'd laugh at her,
chocolate-stuffed child, overripe, absurd.

So she keeps pounding the keys,
secret song always just out of reach.

I hear the music resume.
We are Changeling.
She seeks my tune.

V
The Dance

How then can I ever learn to be,
If I can't find my song and it can't find me?
I search in other people but while searching high and low
find I'm tied to the earth and I can't let go.

We left one country and started life in another,
me my sisters and my mother and my brother.
I left one mask behind and sought another one,
Just one little girl, told her new life had begun.

How then can I ever learn to be,
if I can't find my song and it can't find me?
I search in other people but while searching high and low
find I'm tied to the earth and I can't let go.

I hid my truth it was easier to lie,
weaving pictures of what might be so I didn't have to cry,
left my horse and my dad and the life that I once knew
as my life emptied out, a maiden's body grew.

How then can I ever learn to be,
If I can't find my song and it can't find me?
I search in other people but while searching high and low
find I'm tied to the earth and I can't let go.

My heart, limbs and mind contorted once again
I thought that having sex might help me ease the pain
so I danced that dance and the road just carried on
until a handful of pills nearly ended my song.

How then can I ever learn to be,
If I can't find my song and it can't find me?
I search in other people but while searching high and low
find I'm tied to the earth and I can't let go.

A modern maiden I re-entered the fray
I danced in the night and I danced through the day
my love buried deep, there was none left for me and
with my red shoes tied up tightly told myself I was free.

How then can I ever learn to be,
If I can't find my song and it can't find me?
I search in other people but while searching high and low
find I'm tied to the earth and I can't let go.

VI
Game On

King Pawn forward two
The opening move – all to prove.
In games of strategy and mind all is defined.

Black moves to Queen Pawn one,
the position proffered, easily won.
Do I get sucked in, or recognise the reckoning?

Black/white, day/night
act/don't, can't/won't.
Each shift of position a risked admonition.

Life's dance floor a monochrome map.
No way back. Carry on dancing.
Be the best: risk /reward, failure /success.

Two steps forward and a sudden sideways leap
I seek to tame the game's squares
with a knight's shape.

But it's not the right shape.
So the escape attempt becomes an occupation.
Territory unfairly won.

The chronology of me doesn't match where I'm meant to be.
Yet I hold my position.
Game On.

The Knight leaps, intercepting failed exams,
Redirecting. But the Black Queen
Sweeps up unseen, from the other end.

Culling friend and foe alike
the unexpected strike
shatters expectations anyway.

Isolated now I wait,
deliberate internally where I should be.
Protect and reflect, or move on?

If I reach the other end,
get two queens, it's easier to pretend.
Bright smile, 'Game On.'

Should I castle?
Rook and King exchanged, my back line rearranged.
It may help defensively, but does it fit my strategy?

I look at the Rook, devoid of colour on a bleached square,
realise I don't care,
pick the Tower from the Tarot instead.

Board removed. All things new.

The easy thing would have been to stay,
moving my pieces in the proscribed way
as previous generations have taught.

The Tower is fraught. No meek line-standing,
bystanding with the other taken pieces.
Instead, masonry-exploding, life-imploding kaleidoscopes of
colour.

The cards offer Death's scythe,
vines writhing around Empress enthroned,
while the Fool's cliff-top leap opens the way for
the High Priestess to weave moon's light into a day reborn
No strategy here: just the road less taken, snaking towards a
new dawn.

Can board and deck align?
Cat's eye signage of spirit and mind combining
to mark my way till I ignite, phoenix-bright.

VII
Angels

Tick... Tock
Tick... Tock

The strident note of the clock strikes each second, indefatigable.
Looming sounds strangely echoing, inexorable.

Tick.
Can't see the walls but can feel them.
Tock.
Grey. Why is everything so grey?

Not blackness or whiteness, greyness.
Sealing in, squeezing heart and mind. Not kind.
A fist, denying the light of day.

I look for windows. There are none.
The might of the clock dictates all.

Tick.
Place presumed.
Tock.
World consumed.

It's warm, why is it so warm? They won't tell me.
The angels keep me locked up. God tells them to, of course.
Though as I don't believe in him, he can't really keep me in.

Tick.
Talking, I hear them talking
Tock.
They are stalking my dreams.

Whispering. "Nothing's as it seems."
Part of me is crazy, true.
But I can hear everything. Even you.

And I can see more clearly too.
The angels think they know all things -
because they're in heaven.
But their keys don't unlock anything.

Tick.
Not here below, at least
Tock.
My friend has told me so.

She talks to me all the time,
a feast of strange sounds and sweet airs that delight and
hurt not.

Tick.
But they do hurt.
Tok.
Their lack hurts.

Turns my mind instead to stories of dread:
Headless corpses, bleeding roses.

But though the pills they pay me with keep me ill, still,
in their monochrome, her secret language rises, tells of
that missing puzzle piece; release and Home.

I hear susurrating leaves speak of the clock as time's thief
and how
my heart's drum will beat the way to that summoning, "Come."

Tick
I want to be found
Tock
Put my feet on solid ground.

Don't move, the angels are back.
They're shouting.
The noise, I can't bear the noise.
Their cart clatters, I scream to shatter.

Tick
Reverberating.
Tock.
Ouroboros chasing endlessly.

It's just us again, closer now.
Weave your words. I will come.
Let light's lance pierce the grey, show the way.

Help me chase across crowned trees,
flashing limbs reflected in the running brooks beneath
and find the wind's promised peace.

You've been on the tip of my tongue.
For so long I've felt the brush of your song.
I know you can protect me from the angels,
those terrible angels and the noise and the pain
and God.

VIII
Paid

The spear of unmaking pierces her womb
Bloods seeps into my loom
Price paid.

IX

A Prayer To Mother Shipton

Mother Shipton, prophetess
Hear me and help me, my life is a mess.

I have climbed green-slicked rocks and I have forded rushing
streams,
recognising this mossy, lichen-licked forestscape
as the land from my dreams.

I can feel the weight of years lifting from my shoulders,
while in amongst the scattered boulders I can feel yours.
Shunned, yet welcomed as witch, purveyor of potions and
notions
you saw beyond these Yorkshire vales, searching time's chest for
faraway tales.

The rimy rock drips, cave walls darkly glistening,
lime-hewn rippling so alive I seek faces unseen.
I know you're in, yet not of this place.

As I move deeper underground, the sound of the others muffles,
becoming soft —
until all voices are lost and only the summoning remains.
Tongue-tipping truth cuts through my pain.

Mother Shipton, prophetess
Hear me and help me, my life is a mess.

Someone has left a petrified teddy. Is that for me, to test if I'm ready?
Did you try that too? Using the petrifying well, to turn water to stone, then shattering what you'd created to be on your own?

Did you look to nature to see past your unfortunate stature?
See yourself reflected instead in the wild, whispering wood-wide-web?
That's my plan. I can't stand the weight of myself, so here I am.

Wonderful words from my English degree have been readying me.
Strange airs and sweet sounds telling me I can be found,
that I can shape my surrounds.

As I lower myself onto damp stone, deep enough in to be completely alone,
I weave in a silent plea for a normal life
and a man who'll love me as mother and wife.

I've been ill. You know what I've lost and the cost.
So I'm here, allowing the tip tapping, lime trapping,
petrifying power of dripping water to shape the hour,
demanding the surrender of
that sundered piece. Peace.

Mother Shipton, prophetess
Hear me and help me, my life is a mess.

Leg of frog and eye of newt,
turn my muteness into newness.
Bear's paw, crow's caw
Turn my silence to a roar.
A wisp of sorrow, a wash of blood
Turn the tide on pain for good.

Mother Shipton, prophetess
Hear me and help me, my life is a mess.

Walls washed with five centuries of women's words.
I know your cave is the place to be brave, to put aside my will
and be still.
The power of the feminine petrifying what I've been
while pushing me forward
to what I must know next.

I am, Pain tells me I am.
Your weave tells me I can. I seek my name.

"Come, Madeleine."

X
Valkyrie

"Give us a drag of your fag... So ... what do we think?"
  One sister inhales while the other slurps gin.
"Her poison, will it be food or drink?"

"Well, the half-life avatar took her so far,
but now it's reversed she'll see
there's worse things to be."

Angling for a return of her smokes
The youngest gets caught in her Yamaha's spokes.
As leathered limbs hit the ground an angry growl sounds.

A third figure sighs.
"Come on you guys, this is all by the by."
Ice-blue eyes blaze a warning chill.

Retrench, retract. Two of them act,
ruffled black feathers and biker leathers
remain unscathed. They behave and are still.

Her squabbling siblings subdued, peace ensues.
The Elder shares her take on things while neatly folding back
her wings.
"She must learn to wield her pen as a way to cope with pain."

"So what you're saying..."
The Second pauses, forcing smoky rings between sharpened
incisors,
"Is, being whole will surprise her?"

"Yes," comes the reply, with a hint of a sigh,
"much better for a maiden soul to remain unblooded,
disembodied."

"Ha!" the explosive rejoinder a cackled reminder of the chaos
within,
sinking one hand into her wolf's silver ruff, the Second takes
another puff.

"Her soul may be sweet, but her modern maid's flesh is weighed
and found wanting."

Lightening crackles in the voice of the blonde. No longer
blazing, her eyes look beyond.

"Silence. That's how she lost her song. Too soon, too young.
She's the warrior one, the unsung hero survivor we will deliver,
eventually."

Having reclaimed her cigarette, the copper-haired youngest
exhales regret.

"We can't take her now, she needs to learn how to forgive, to live.
But when she's properly back together, we'll come to collect and
she'll be with us forever."

"I agree, she's too heavily laden to bear the title of maiden.
So for now she's alone," the Second intoned.

"Her warrior's field the marriage bed and her quest
love unbound as a thread to be found, but we owe her a debt."

"The pain will drive her to the brink, remember....?"

A pregnant pause as they think.

Not birthed by a virgin earth, they know their survival needs
new arrivals.
In return for cessation of pain, they gather the slain.
Accompanied by flocks of rooks they sort the craven from the
brave.

Going back to the question, the youngest lightens the mood.
"I reckon food. She's already eating more than before. Her
weight hides her,
provides her with something to blame when it all feels insane."

"We'll leave her for now. Agreed?"
Shrugged resignation accompanies nodded assent.
They all know what is meant.

Though the Second understands the injections prevent
contraception she sees the futility of being contrary. Says
simply,
"If she breeds, she'll find love's seed."

Then joins with her sisters as they say,
"Today the pain will burn, the world will turn –
But tomorrow her man comes and she'll become."

"Well then, till we meet again."

Moment captured. Scene fractures.
The Valkyrie have places to be.

INTERLUDE I

My Gift To You Is Silence

My gift to you is silence
its golden, tear stained glory
is not hate-stained or pain-stained
because its beacon, unsullied and bright,
is held in the amber of my backbone.

You will never know what it is costing me
to keep the secret lost in me
so you stay in the light.

But as you often remind me
truth has a habit of doubling back.
So one day and despite my best efforts
the whip of its tail may still find you.

PART TWO
MOTHER

I

The Beginning Of Things

She's looking at me, what does she see?
Blazing halo, white whings replacing raven flutterings,
a crossed sword and shield shadowing green fields?

A lead and glass angel, I illuminate the altar
glass-refracting, light-directing colours
beaming rainbows onto the bowed heads below.

This tableau of sacrifice and slaughter is something I
understand.
The blood of the lamb poured out onto the land to reshape,
regenerate.
But for me and my sisters it's not just the once.

We bleed with the moon and the seasons.
No father and son, just life and death – both hard won.
I'm from an older Trinity, here shifted to Christianity.

As I look down past the raised thorn crown, I purposely widen
my field of vision
to encompass the font and beyond.
A golden boy struggles in her arms.
Over the head of the dutiful flock our gaze locks.

Looking alarmed, the priest in white glances at the tall man on
his right,
hoping his fatherhood presence can prevent impending
accidents. It works.
Under the force of parental will, the ten-month-old stills.

Water-cupped wet-slicked curls.
I feel the spirit unfurling. In me and of me.
In this hour I'm the conduit of power.

Warmth floods. The atmosphere unexpectedly shifting,
a spiritual homecoming lifting other burdens away.
The congregation thinks this feeling comes from Son through
glass.

But it's me and I'm not held fast in those haloed colours.
Fractured by light, my spirit bright takes wing.
I'm the Elder Valkyrie changing shape to what She sees.

She, the seeker of the unknown, hungering for a spell that
rectifies,
a propitiation of pain to rise beyond memory's stain
in a way that can be managed, isn't damaged.

She'd wanted to flee, told her husband to set her free.
The third time she'd demanded it, he did. Then, trying to go
back and —
finding herself supplanted, she'd needed to dig up the new roots
he'd planted.

Look at them go, seemingly steady, ready to do what it takes.
It's not quite fake, despite protestations there is love there.
She doesn't know how, doesn't care. But it's fractured.

Family broken; her prayers spoken in different places to other
faces
seeking hope in sky and cards where the dark can gain hold if
the pain is too stark.
There was no release. So now she's in church, seeking peace.

I am. Her pain tells me I am.
As they sing the final song her will is so strong I can feel myself change,
her presence moulding me into a shape that fits the godhead she expects to see.

My sword wielded steadily, I'll slash at the ties that bind her subconscious mind.
She'll reach that place in herself, where she can find herself.
And that little boy, the first of three, will help her wield her poetry.

Not as Other, but Mother.

II
Shop Windows

I look, trying to find myself.
The first glance I caught of myself
walking past an earlier window was not encouraging.
'Fat bitch.'

Trying again, I stop in front of another,
also filled with dressed dummies touting their wares.
"Mummy, stop staring. I want an ice-cream!"
Screaming inside I ignore both voices and keep looking.

I snort in derision at how my hoped-for look-see is thwarted by
the real me.
How the hanging belly-bulging flesh of this mirrored comic
shape
keeps firmly forcing softly billowing breasts into my line of
vision.

I will my mind to free itself and look in askance at the
passers-by for help,
wondering if they can see beyond the me I've spent thirty years
perfecting.
But they don't bat an eye at my disfigured figure.

Focus drifting, I don't notice my two-year-old's frantic shifting
from one leg to another.
But I do hear, "Bother!" and look down to see a puddle
pooling in an alarming way around the new shoes she chose
today.

A wide grin plasters itself over her older brother's face.
He's enjoying her disgrace and I'm compelled to move on,
seek out loos, change clothes and shoes.

I rinse things out, risking a glimpse into the mirror above the
sink.
I try not to shrink away from the full moon face, balloon jaw.
But instead, the waxy pallor of a new moon sliver confronts me,
quivering lip stretching bravely into the semblance of a smile.

It's been a while since I've managed one of those.
It's odd. When I had the operation and lost ten stone
I expected size twelve clothes to help me atone for the fatter me.

But that was sight unseen. With Christmas just gone,
a yoghurt pot my festive treat —
I can't see beyond the mountain of flesh enmeshed with my
soul.
It's as though it's kept me whole.

My daughter now presentable, I plop her back into the buggy.
My son is being particularly huggy, revelling in his sister's
lamentable state.
We push back into the frantic, bargain-hunting crowd.

A series of jerks and clicks and a woebegone wail tell me I've left
the breaks on.
I search my handbag to keep 'baby' happy, find something sweet
and a 'just in case' nappy.
When I look up, I'm face-to-face with a plastic-legged torso,
encased in purple leather.

I find the price tag, along with the size tag – wrong price, perfect size.
Maybe it's enough to know they'd fit me now.
That despite what I see in the glass, girl-mountain-me is a thing of the past.

I feel him before I see him. A six-foot presence, making up for the absence I feel in myself.
"Why not try them on? Look, they're in the sale." I push past my self-disgust to look at him, sensing how he's willing me to see myself as he does.

I quail, but then put aside my qualms and with a calm I
don't feel
take a size twelve off the shelf and head to the changing rooms.
Pulling the curtain across I focus on buttons and zips, realise how what I'm wearing doesn't fit.
Loosely hanging clothes swamp me, no longer belonging on my much-too-small frame.

There is a pain in this passing. But when I do finally look up, I realise there's joy in this shape,
and despite the deep red scar running through it, start admiring my new waist.
As I fasten the last button, I feel the purple leather moulding me into a new entity.

I cry. Then head held high, walk out for my family to see.
A short while later we leave the cocooning warmth of the shop, I'm sporting a new top too. My husband insisted; it's Rangers' blue.

As the four of us wait for the bus, I notice the glass of the shelter.

38

Oddly, my reflected hair shimmers copper red and, for a fleeting moment,
I could swear that instead of closed shop blinds I see wings
fanning out behind.

I know I'm seeing things, but so much has changed,
my life rearranged –
so why not black feathers and purple biker leathers?

III
Kirmes

Mouths where they shouldn't be
tongue where it shouldn't be
but this time it's not me.

Painted eyes, clown's face, red mouth,
horses flying, cars running, children riding,
round and round goes the merry-go-round, a jarring sound.

Gingerbread hearts, broken hearts, parts in pieces, plastic toys,
ceaseless noise overflowing. I've had enough.
Round and round, lost and found, a jarring sound.

Mouths where they shouldn't be
tongue where it shouldn't be
thumb in mouth plugged. That's me.

She's on his lap. Küsschen, Mäuschen. My Little Miss.
I gag. I want to gouge, scream, slap.
Instead, with childhood's fingers down my throat, I choke.

Then with a tinkling sprinkling of magic dust rust the sounds
stop.
The fairground ride bids us inside. Princess promise, rubies and
gold, story untold.
The magpie perches as the carriage lurches and we move
forward.

She picks up the reins of our coach's steed, "Giddy up horsey!"
We gather speed.
Kicking legs up the momentum and she shrieks with delight
"Whoosh!"
I pick up the refrain when I notice it's a wolf, not horse,
pulling us.

I will it into being: spell-carved metal and plastic into
teeth-ripping life.
Though our direction of travel is circular, so we're not going far,
I start feeling alive. The grimace I've plastered over my face is
slipping.

Faster and faster it goes. I am, pain tells me I am.
Together now we hold the reins, my head screams that I can.

The wolf turns, snarling. The Wild is calling.

Mouths where they shouldn't be. I'm seeing and not seeing,
child's innocence eclipses fleeing memories.
Tongue where it shouldn't be, it's slippery-wet darkness
gnawing at me.

I scream to end the noise in my head
but am still surprised when my child slides off my knee.
She wants to be somewhere else instead.

Called by drip-fanged golden-eyed glory
I follow my daughter outside to sit astride.
A full-throated roar sounds as the wolf form shatters.

My red clown mouth clatters to the painted wooden floor.
I realise that the mouth where it shouldn't be and tongue where
it shouldn't be isn't my fault. I finally see.
The she-wolf has risen from her prison.

I scream out my pain. NEVER AGAIN.
Fingers sinking into fur tease out crystal clarity.
I lose myself, trying to loose myself. Deeper and deeper.
My child self didn't know that wasn't how it was s'posed to go.
I hold my daughter tight. I will fight. I am protector and keeper.

Then it stops. It all stops. There is violence in the silence.

We step off together, first holding hands but then she's
running away from the woman who roared,
back into the distorted land from before.

I prepare to put my clown's smile back in place,
attempt to pretend
there's nothing extraordinary here, that it's all as it should be.
But then I look at her disappearing figure and know she's
depending on me.

My fear is sick-making, jaw-breaking. I'm turned inside out. Still
I roar its finish.
For so long, forgetting what he stole, I allowed my childhood to
burn into adulthood.
But my mind is now whole and I'm no longer diminished. The
world turns.

I pluck forest memories of garlanded green from the sticky
August air.
Suffocating, cloying, debilitating becomes permeable, light and
invigorating.

Kirmes stands for Church Mass: an inaugural celebration from
earlier times.
But as I hear the town clock chime, I know the shadows here are
older still.
Threading my will into the fabric of things I pray to whatever is
here, to hear.

As Kingdom-encompassing spirit-warmth pushes outwards
a single feather drifts to the ground.
I examine the black and white perfection of Nature's message,
telling me that just for today I'm OK.

I look in the funhouse mirror and see my image repeating
infinitely.
Multiple versions of me frame a ghost train carriage passing into
a tooth-fanged maw.
Swallowed whole it goes into the black. There's no turning back.

That night, my last one under his roof I sink myself bone claw
and tooth into staying aloof.
I love him still; the mad man living in a parody home, who
despite his wife is all alone.
Has he already atoned? I drink glass after glass of sparkling
wine. The bubbles tell me I'm fine.

The next morning we leave. As our engine roars
I tighten she-wolf claws around my world.
I am Mother not meat. My cubs are freed.
I allow my memories to bleed all over the car.

A magpie caws.

IV

I want to drown in their laughter
I want their kisses to smother me
I want their tears to stab me
I want their smiles to pierce me
while the memory of their sweet-smelling skin lacerates mine.

And when I leave in the morning I need to tell myself that it's
not a long time
until I see them again.

© a working Mum

V
Three Pieces Of Glass

The train crunches up the line,
each turn of the wheel marking time
over and over again.
Deep breath in. I count to ten.

Dirt-streaked glass bars me from the outside.
Staying the course is a matter of pride. And money.
For six months I'm a shadowed creature of the dark,
so unused to the sun that even when it shines I cower
in the phony luxury of my dirty velveteen seat.
Yet one and all, we follow London's call.

On one hand it's the promised land, but it's also pitiless,
mocking my distress.
I secretly hope it will spit me out, but am not quite sure how to
bring this about.
This track holds my way back home. Deep breath out.
Miles crunching past the failed business, broken ego, words
spoken in haste.
The superglue paste I hope will put it all back together again –
a salary – will set me free, we said. That's why I'm on this train.
But all I see from 5.50 'till 8 is blurred coloured flashes,
in waves, dots and dashes flying past my window pane.

In a bid to allay my worries and troubles,
I lace my orange squash with bubbles.
It started on my journey home, when I first got paid,
but increasingly they're easing the start of my day.

A squash bottle, seen through other people's eyes
is a great disguise for what's really inside.
I decant from a never-ending parade of glass bottles.
Discarded sharp-edged shards ripping through bins.
I wonder whether anyone else gets hurt.
Meanwhile, I'm fine. I have wine.

I look for the genie in the bubbles, soothing, smoothing,
promising serenity.
I know it's not there, but as time is pressing and I'm still
stressing, I surrender my cares.
The train crunches up the line, each turn of the wheel marking
time.

I forget what I need, allowing myself to bleed into the vine,
wondering whether this will help the root bear fruit.
I see the inside of the glass reflected and so, with my gaze now
directed past
tables and chrome, I watch the light from our phones illuminate
us hungry ghosts.
Gladrags and designer bags transformed from what we want
most, to rags.

To prove I'm OK, I copy the other commuters and open my
computer.
Just another piece of glass. Here the world moves even faster:
Informationnewsdisaster, doitnowbutIdontknowhow,
Ihavewhatyouwantgiveitapunt, youcunt.

I move past the bright-beamed streaming to the pixels proving
I'm here.
Navigate my way through the likes to the emailed notes,
convoluted tropes and cardboard clichés. My inbox tells me I
matter
and helps me ignore the clatter of a world falling apart.
While the waves of my mind crash against my heart,
bubbles burst around the hurt, making me brave.
As I feel it shatter it into a thousand pieces I vaguely wonder
whether in time, it will turn to sand. Another sip of wine.
I'm fine.

I can't bear the screen any more, so pretend to rest.
Making my final push for peace I invest in the last minutes left.
But my mind's eye can't see past the mountains of glass.
Uncountable shards slicing the world into a glasscaped
desert landscape I can't seem to escape.

As my head spins, I try to pin my mind by fixing on something.
But even here I slip.
A broken bottle sends me on a full throttle slide down the hill,
spilling blood and guts.
I rip as I tip over curved bottle bottoms and necks and sides.
Eventually, I slide across a mosaic floor of glass panes.
Mesmerised, I watch pieces stretch into infinity
each angled shape reflecting glimpses of me, bits of myself
shifting under my feet.

This killer kaleidoscope offers no succour. I suffer.
Hear my fear beating in counterpoint to the train's crunching,
heart punching through my chest. I want to wake. But the glass
is too fast.
It's fake, spinning me around, pinning me with the tantalising
promise of:
"Just round the corner" and, "You're getting warmer…"
I dare to glimpse down, hoping to see a way past this
slippy-sliding inside-outing
world-colliding vertigo. But there's nowhere to go.

Time slows as faces flash:
"Mummy," drink one to atone.
"Can I stay up when you come home?"
"You're not good enough." I call my boss' bluff, and drink more.
"You've failed," I hear, and there goes number four.
My stinking thinking is relieved by drinking.

I'm trying to climb out of my dream but slip back.
Time and time again glass cuts into my skin.
I can feel the slivers slicing soles and palms when
suddenly shrieking breaks push me out of harm's way.

Movement stops. Back in the present I glance around;
no-one has noticed my absence. I check myself, nothing broken.
The pigeons pecking on the platform beckon. Doors slide open.
St Pancras International, the world of the rational.
My day has begun.

A glint catches the corner of my eye. They're there, shining.
The feathers, the leathers and the copper hair
a glory-transfigured triptych to help me see.
I feel in my bones it's a sign. Smeared glass vanquished,
I take their direction, facing what is to come head on.

49

VI
My Little Candle Flame
(From a Daughter to her Mother)

My little candle flame so soft and sweet,
my little candle flame gently quivers to the beat.
This little flame so delicate and gentle
as a little raindrop in no rage.
My little candle flame as movement touches
my little candle flame as things get tough.

With a little excitement, with sadness too,
this little light keeps shining on you.
With carelessness and caring
with being sensible and daring
don't go wandering into the wilderness with temptation too.

My Little Candle Flame
(From a Mother to her Daughter)

My little candle flame is very, very small,
my little candle flame is hardly there at all.
The wilderness has got too wild
temptation runs too deep,
but your little candle flame stops mine from going to sleep.
That and the love of our family
have given me strength to try to fight free.

God says just call and you shall be healed
and light will blaze over all that once was concealed.
Your little candle flame keeps me alight
it stops mine from going into the night.

So keep blazing my darling with joy, hope and love
and your little candle flame will stay lit from above.

VII
Coming Home

"I'm not what I was, look at my wings
They're bright white and these other things... You too!"
The Elder looks at her sisters, her halo askew.
"And all these bloody white doves, what can we do?"
Gesticulating wildly, she sweeps their flutterings away.
They coo.

"It's driving me mad! Do you think it's because she's not so sad
anymore?
Well, she is. But you know what I mean. She saw us when we
appeared.
But then something interfered. Unexpectedly
it redirected our truth. Then it lifted and she shifted."

The Youngest nods sagely,
"She saw us vaguely, but there was something else.
Maybe she saw herself?"

The Second replies. "Well, she'd tried suicide
and didn't die, so what were we supposed to do?"
The wolf snarls on cue.
"Yes dear, we were right to show ourselves.
But it was Him, He interfered again!
He's causing her to see a different Trinity."

"When He hung on the cross it all changed.
Odin's tree rearranged. And yet..."

The Youngest speaks regret,
"The All-Father was the first to hang.
That's when our world still gave a damn."

"And don't forget, he rose again,
suffering aeons of pain and
it took nine days, not three!
"Sacrificing an eye, falling on a spear to die,
then the hanging."

There is anger and danger.
The Second chokes as her wolf howls.
Fenrir's voice sounding a warning
as black ravens scythe through the doves.

"But he did it for self, not love…"

In another place she hears. Not knowing she's to blame
for the Valkyrie's shame, the woman lifts her face.
She senses something pervading this place.

Shifting her position, the floor hard on her knees,
she puts her hands together in a supplicant's plea.
"I want to hope and if it's in your gift,
please lift this sense of fear that traps me here."

Today she's all alone, in her new bungalow home.
It's not far for the kids to come and go, she knows.
But her family's decreased to three over four days a week.
The hole in her heart grows.

She wants to leave herself at the foot of His cross.
Use it to cross those dimensions of loss to another place.
Find healing and that feeling that she's back in control, whole.
Surely, she's spilt enough blood: mind, body and soul?

She wants forgiveness, an end to pain,
but knowing it's sure to come back again
she continues to seek. Like any other hungry ghost.

Then, last night, as she lay in her bed,
a vision dripped down from the ceiling.
She finally begged, exhaling a whispered, "protect."

It had some effect, so she's here.
On her knees. No beer or wine.
Admitting she's not fine she
prays for a God of her understanding.

"If He died for our sins as a man,
can His place of birth not be the universe
reshaped into a dragoned female form?
Fiery natural power, begotten, not made.
Then rise as God, price paid?"

The hamster squeaks and she turns to the garden.
Even working from home he's a burden,
yet she's pleased he's here.
An unexpected urgency sends her to his cage by the window.

First she unlatches it, then finds herself opening the patio door.
Outside now, she pushes her hand into the straw,
Goldie's sharp teeth find her soft-fleshed thumb. Release.
She watches him run, a pale streak though the long grass.

It's so fast she almost misses the rustle of feathers
silent wings descending upon a garden undefended.
It strikes. Razored beak blooded,
golden eyes hooded, a ball of fur, talon-held.
Breaking the spell, the sparrow hawk takes flight.

One white underfeather remains.
With kill fulfilled, is this fluff from the bird
a sign she's been heard?
Something shifts inside.
Bare feet on grass. This is the hour.

A vast power unfurls,
it burns to the bone.
Mother's calling her home.

VIII
Dragon

I am. Endless coils, shimmering, blinking,
winking in and out
not Deceiver,
but in the eye of the perceiver,
there's no room for doubt that I am.

I am. Undulating bronze and gold, binding
and unwinding constantly
I breathe desire
explode with fire,
there is consistency to my entropy. I am.

I am both beginning and ending
making worlds as the Word.
Ouroboros, Serpent,
Mother of all things.
Life bringing, death singer. I am.

Harbringer, sum of all that is and was
I am all-seeing.
No because. Just being.
My womb's safedark
Ignites the spark. I am.

A milky streak in the black,
placental abruption
an afterbirth of stars
the creation of earth.
A membranous veil between
its birth blood and my blood.

When the first Word was spoken
one became all and all became nothing.
But I created people to fill it –
stone, flesh and spirit
to do the things I couldn't do.
But now, creation has fallen to to you.

What will you do?
You used your poetry to call to me.
I replied with train and hawk
and the grace-given, reshriven Valkyrie.
They've set you free, by the way.

So, act and write what you've seen,
share the places you've been.
Translate your truth through poetry;
you'll help others see all that is and shall be.
Believe and transcend.

Don't bear the weight of aeons alone,
the world is shaped with kisses, not stones.
Open your heart, my Son did his part
on the cross. His sacrifice, the price.
The resurrection of him through me
is the connection to set you free.

You'll claim your place
in my Queendom;
it's the gift of freedom.
No beginning or end
to protect or defend.

So, open your will and be still.
draw from the earth,
stop withholding your worth.

Tail in maw, I spin.
Bird song, raven's caw, lion's roar —
I'm chasing stories from glory to glory,
an endless figure of eight.

Look into the water my daughter,
the world unseen is in reach.
My eyes reflected in changeable skies.
Clouds whirling as the world turns,
I teach all things and nothing.

Find me in pixels and cat's tails and lichen,
fissured rocks and fission, guns and rape,
the wars you make, the lives you take.
The renewal comes after each fall.

Mothers of the hereafter,
call me Father if you must
but trust in a life of love
walk the way of my Son.

The world turns as my breath burns.
When you're ready to know me, name me.
You'll feel me beckon. I am Dragon.

IX
Sacrifice

I am in Her place, I see His face
I no longer kneel but lie on the cold stone floor –
leave myself on the cross as I walk through the door.

Glorious now I arise.
Will sacrificed.

X
Just For Today

Today I'm very frightened
I'm full of fear today,
the things I thought defined me
have upped and gone away.
Redundancy has left a hole
gaping in my Soul
and all the things I thought made me
are not what make me whole.

A Title, a Name, a Game
a Job, a Chair and Blame
I know a salary does not equal me
but what does?

Is it the knowing I must find out
what my life's all about
making me frightened?

No Comfort Cushion, Emails, Fake Smiles
to derail or defocus
just me.
So, how will I be?

Today I will write of the moon and the stars
and the smell of my daughter's hair
as I prepare her for her school trip.

Today I will enjoy seeing love renewed in my husband's eyes
as he looks at me, reassuring me it's all alright,
it's just a blip, I'll find something soon.

Today I will start on a frame-work
wrought from the love and hope that defines who I am.
I will listen to the deep, throbbing sound of the drums of Your
will that tell me I can.

So, just for today I shall:

Share the Thought that compels
the Truth that cuts through
the Beauty that shines
and the Good that is You.

Today I'm very frightened,
but I am not Afraid.

XI
A Mother's Blessing

Let your eyes be the light
let your arms be a hug
let your mouth be a whispered kiss of hope;
and let your ears hear the love I spoke
to my Little Miss in her crib (meinem Bub in seiner Wiege).

Let your feet take you forward,
let your head keep you back
from the mistakes I once made.

And do not be afraid.
This journey you're on
will be a song of joy
in the pits of despair,
a dance of courage
on ground so rare it will break your heart with its beauty.

You don't know, is my point –
and won't until you're on the path.

But hold on to the love you are given,
to the love you give and the strength you have.
Own what you live.

Your path is your path
and your way is your way
live it today.

INTERLUDE II

I'm Sorry

I'm so sorry you had to worry
about what I was going to do next.
The subtext of each action
fractioned by your teenage mind,
trying to work out
who I was and where.

I understand why you wanted to run
as far away from me as you could.
I did try to follow, but a hollow-legged,
pity meander left me stumbling and floundering.

I made it in the end, holding you close.
But to you my embrace was a noose,
frightening in its tightening.
So you watched me every day
thinking I'd give way until finally,
you started to trust.

You'd always loved, but knowing that now
my comings and goings were safe and protected,
your life unaffected, you started to believe
in the reprieve of a life redirected.

Those broad shoulder of yours
didn't need to hold up the world anymore.
But the Atlas of a man you'd become
wasn't able to shrink back to the boy
who'd bathed in the sun of innocence.

Will my sorries ever be enough to fill the giant form you
assumed, completing the places I should have been?
Motherhood is not a given, it needs to be earned
So now I use my life to show I've learned love Is enough.

PART THREE
CRONE

I
The Flight of the Crone

It started with a stye on my eye that wouldn't go.
I watched with horror as it raced to displace
the spiderweb lines life had etched on my face.

In my late forties, I'd long made peace with my reflection,
my quest for perfection released. But this carbuncle,
pressure-grown, shaped the familiar flow of me quite
differently.

There had once been pleasure in being sky woman, fly woman,
jumping-on-a-plane-woman, accepting-the-pain-woman,
in-control-wise-woman, moving-past-all-woman.

I'd convinced myself there was power in purpose
so squeezed every last drop from my bones
when I really just longed to be home.

As silver-silk flight paths spun their threads past
the Middle East and Africa, Sweden, Scotland, then south east
England,
it was comforting knowing that my comings and goings
mattered.

I would work to push down pain and, every time it rose again,
despite being shattered, jump on another plane.
I knew I was tough, but it was never enough.

The doctor said the flying and trying to complete my endless
lists had caused the cyst he'd cut out. But then my eye was OK,
and I continued on in just the same way;
countries and faces interchangeable,
projects increasingly unsustainable.

But in that secret part of me, I'd buried inadvertently more
pressure points pushed.
My dragon's teeth, grown from sliced-through 'shoulds' and
'oughts' wrought truth.
So, the next time my boss said go, I said no.

I shared my last drive from the airport to coast with a host of
birds.
Ghosting through the blue predawn they dropped off one
by one,
until it was just me and the herring gull chasing a rising sun.

Following this golden-eyed, blazing-white predator through
sky-washed pink,
made me think how he'd had to adapt to the meagre portion we
left him.
His fish-filled sea becoming snatched-from-plate, people-food.

And we people approached with caution, circumventing his
terrain staked
with fierce, full-throated calls. So profound was this sound that,
on this last drive home –
its remembered energy caused my name to ring through me
repeatedly.

I prayed for days. Walking with nature, waxing and waning
until the fiercer me was in ascendancy. I continued to pray,
walking some more, past wild waves and fractured shores.

There was exhilaration in watching the creation of each
moment.
And the more grounded I became, the more willing I was
to feel the pain and let my story unfold.

This was the time to be bold. The soft thrumming of a wider
will changing me from flight woman to fight woman. But I could
still be still. And in the silence
I recognised power moving from human-handed violence, into
something else.

I started running, loving the pounding soles of my orange
trainers on the welcoming sand,
sounding out a new life begun.
As the world flashed past, I finally understood nothing could
last.

———

Another day, another gull. My heart is full as I see the winged M
silhouetted
against the evening sky. I watch it fly and think of when I was
far from home,
how where I've flown and the people I've known, all embody the
flight of the crone.

I'll convey what we need to say. Not poetry yet, but instead
cast my net with silver-tongued prose.
My book will be filled with glorious tales,
victorious voices unveiled will paint love's consummation.

I'll weave pixels into promises and shared words into prayers of
hope,
and so transform this world of men to somewhere crones can fly
again.

II
The Telephone Consultation

"Yes, I'm Covid free."

"No, no continuous cough or loss of taste."
Such a waste last time. Not that it's had much of an impact on
my waist line, but still."

"Yes, hot flushes and anxiety."
"Daily, oh most definitely. And it's getting worse."

"External factors? I'm in overload! Stuff's coming at me from
everywhere. Feels like I'm cursed."

"We've two adult kids away from us. They're stuck in different
cities in their rabbit-hutch flats.
And my youngest didn't sit her GCSEs and Mum's got Covid-
caused heart disease... well you get the idea."

"How's it made me feel? It's all quite surreal, more like a
nightmare or dream."
"Not that I'm sleeping much. Keep waking up."

"Worried! Well, I'm sorry, but wouldn't you be after what I've
shared? I want to be there, but don't know where I'm needed.
So everything's superseded by an ever-present panic."

"Yes, I know we're coming out of things, but it still feels like
both roundabouts and swings are vying for my attention."

"You're right to mention it all seems a bit frantic. Hence my
request for HRT!"

"What's that you say? Something stronger, that might last longer? No, I definitely don't want any anti-depressants. I've had them before and don't want any more!"

"They're like a cushioned barrier stopping my words from flowing and me from knowing what I can and can't do."

"Yes, and I exercise too! A run and a ride most every day keeps the doctor away, supposedly.
Though, my horse has lots to say about my recent lack of time. She thinks it's linked to a sharp decline in my spirits…"

"No, she doesn't really talk, but pouring tears and ideas into her mane helps me stay sane. It's all relative, isn't it?"

"An example of things that have happened? My book launch last year and all that entailed made me feel like I'd failed. It was supposed to be big and in Canada, where the publishers are. Instead, Covid and lockdown meant very few sales."

"Yes, it was hard. Writing it took a year of my life with lots of financial sacrifice. Despite writing with purpose and the best of intent, I didn't really understand what all of it meant. Though I'm now more aware of the writer's lament!"

"That iron will, those nerves of steel aren't about the writing or the plot reveal. It's when you realise your work might be nothing, or that you've left out the crucial bit that might turn it into something."

"Absolutely. The sense of failure that entailed nearly sent me back to the bottle. Instead, I used food which was nearly as good. Or bad, depending on your perspective. Though, the constant sugar hits did make me feel like shit."

"Apologies, I didn't mean to swear. But yes. That's about the sum of it."

"No, I don't think my need for HRT is based on bad eating habits."

"Am I satisfied with this consultation? Well Doctor, it's not as though you've prescribed anything yet. Though I live in hope."

"What do you mean? You can't? Why ever not, when I've shared the full scope of my needs?"

"I know there's a shortage but surely there must be some advantage to having the history I do.
Can't I jump the queue?"

"I've made you smile. Well, that's good, but what comes next?"

"You'll pass me over to the doctor to be seen? I'm perplexed. If you're not a GP, what has this been?"

"But as a triage nurse, there must be something you can try?"

"OK, OK. I do believe your hands are tied. I'll wait for the call, do as you say. No bother at all."

"So how long d'you think I'll have to wait?"

"A week. So, next week Thursday from eight? Yes, I'll have my phone on."

"Just a moment, can you hold on? A panic attack.... Yes, I'm nearly done."

"Hello, hello? Have you gone?"

———

The silence from my phone is deafening.
Maybe I just wasn't ready to say
that I really haven't been well today, or any other day.
And that,
even though most restrictions are gone now, I've forgotten how
to be a part of things, preferring to be apart from things.

While I'm being polite and making the person at the other end
feel like a friend,
the forced bonhomie makes it hard to relate the struggle in me;
to tell of the fear-and-failure-rats clawing and gnawing at my
essence.
I still myself, praying for the strength of will to be myself.

I won't let dull hard resignation diminish me. Instead,
I'll remember that,
in times past, being nothing, has sometimes allowed me to be
all things.
I'll wait; fate's flaming sword will set me free.
And if not, there's HRT.

III
A House Full of Kids

I once had a house full of kids, dears
the most exuberant bunch in the world.
There were mud-splattered boots in the hall, dears
and drama and dance for the girls.

Then number one left for Scotland
and number two, near London town
and then there were three in the house, dears
and we started to double down.

Now three have turned into two, dears
as another one moves away
the images left mere ghosts, dears
of brim-full yesterdays.

With a film of dust on the shelves, dears
behind yellowing, slightly smeared glass
the paintings they did on the fridge, dears
from a time that went too fast.

And then, when the house is empty
just the two of us filling this place
we chase shadows of those who once lived here
through an altogether new time and space.

But instead of misty-eyed missing
and hollowly echoing walls
we'll remember that as creators
of that life, we can find our way to new shores.

Adventure and travel and hope, dears
in each other and the ones who have left
and rather than bemoaning their lack, dears
complete once again, not bereft.

And our house will be full of more kids, dears
a joyous and happy new world.
With us sitting right in the middle
as the next life's chapter unfurls.

IV
Entangled

There are mushrooms in my garden, they're poking through
the lawn
I'm out today quite early, I love gardening at dawn.

The colours are more vivid and everything seems new
I feel tremendous energy, cascading up and surging through.

But despite their mayfly fragility, in this world directed by me
these fungal invaders are not what I'd hoped to see this
morning.

Last night as I'd stood in this place, a full-bodied moon
bathing my face, a howl arose.
It felt too much, so I squashed it. Instead casting silent tones
upwards.

Is this new fairy-ring a reminder of last night's awakening?
Earth's answering call to loneliness unspoken and loved ones far
from home?

Thoughts turn to the fecund borders and the comforting order
of my carefully tended world.
Here among the noise of thrusting shoots and root-feeding
aphids, I'm heard.

I'm pleased I've remembered to put on crocs over my socks. I
often forget when
rushing out to clear overnight detritus or free budding plants
seeking light.

I'm on the grass, marvelling at the cream-headed multitude
when energy shoots through me. I sense familiarity.

It's like the shape I become when I'm riding my mare and I feel
no fear.
I see life in the sward and the hawk on the post.
Our bond is stronger than most.

Barefoot now and stock still, I wonder at the strength of this
sense while away from her.
Are the mycelial strands in this here and now nature's response
to my moon-shot howl?

As above so below. Earth's whispered breath, telling me to
follow her manifest,
go beyond that place of loneliness into a wider connectedness to
find rest.

I allow the world unseen to pull at me, feel my feet sink through
the grass.
The head-spinning new reality moves fast, swallowing all of me.

I understand this early spring patch of green is reality seen,
but am emboldened by an earth-enfolding mind's-eye way of
seeing.

It's as though, up until now, a mind-full blindfold has stopped
me. But waking up to the secrets of this land, I'm able to draw
what's been asleep up and into my hands.

I recognise these patterns now. The woven order in my pots and
borders are ideas remembered, showing me how to turn this
mad terrain into my domain.

I allow myself to become entangled and am reminded I don't always need to see the threads of life cocooning me, and that things don't always happen because of patterns.
It's a womb, not a tomb.

I think of the fluidity of life's demands on me. My surface thoughts a tiny fraction of this interaction. As above, so below. Do I reap what I sow?

Chaos demands attention, calls for a different direction.
As below so above. I must let go with love.

Consciousness wakes. Centaur self in the ascendant, I'm no longer dependent on what others think.
I will fall and break but can rewrite both the spoken and unspoken to remake what is broken.

A deep joy speeds my toiling hands to pastures new.
Nothing is spoilt.
I marvel at the strands of life held in my garden's microcosm.

With ivy and bindweed outracing true blossoming, I prune and cut back for hours.
I'm proud I've survived to become this I am. In moving past pain I've found pardon.

As I work my soul sings, accepting this new shape of things, including the mushrooms.
I let my senses unravel. There is no perfection, just direction of travel.
With the sun now riding high, I launch new words into the sky.

V

Watercolour Days

Our world is one of watercolours
seeping into each other,
blended waves and frequencies
shaping what we see.

White is the absence of colour,
sitting as light it defines the others.
The alpha and omega of a spectrum
based on perception.

Red's conclusion marks pink's beginning, rain's end.
But as warming yellows yolk
into dazzling motes of orange, overspilling,
we often remain remote from these bursting colour notes.

Instead we clash, crash and bounce;
people passing along, moving back and forth,
paths constantly intersecting. Discrete like dodgem cars
we're oblivious to the rainbow-hued blues
shooting through water that pools on grey pavements.

Most of the time in a world flashing past
the lack of chain reaction interactions goes unnoticed.
But today there's a shift in focus.
Light's interplay becoming truth
makes this a watercolour kind of day.

Blue paints the space between her and me.
Cool like water, hot like flame, it's wash a butterfly's breath.
Not long enough to punctuate or be set on a page
but its wings unleash energy; revealing, healing.

Mirrored in her eyes,
I'm part of these watercolour skies
a blue-hued aura as far as the eye can see
spreading across flora and fauna.
In seeing her, I see me.

Then the veil draws over again.
We discuss the weather and whether its better
to put goats or sheep out with the horses.
We're two middle aged women soaked by rain
in a world moved back to the mundane.

I try to create new watercolour days by writing.
But despite eyes that are open, they stay away.
So hoping to make myself heard through words seen,
I turn poetry pictures into a book on my shelf.

It's eighteen months on. Imposter syndrome entrenched
and faith entangled, a speaker feeds my soul from the pulpit.
Painting over my sit-on-the-fence poor-me self-portrait
with colours of her own, she allows me to see the girl in
bare feet
who made herself heard by shouting in church. Her truth
eviscerates.

As we hug, a conflagration of warmth enters stone walls,
rivalling the light-shot windows above. Shadows flee and I see
myself
reflected in mossy streams and darkly glossed seaweed greens.
The viscous density of love falls on the congregation, while
orange,
the colour of leadership, leaks light into the world beyond.

To live each day as a watercolour day, I must be part of that.

VI
Spellsong

I draw breath and know what's coming next.
This song is already half-written,
coming unbidden to me last night.
Drip dripping words filling me,
till they're ready to free themselves
from where they're held.

I'm just a temporary resting place,
their power depends on my faith and
it's not a given this equals religion.

In this wildwood world of ours
Christ rides on the wind and howls
his delight at the lost souls found.

He's in this place, but so is She,
there's femininity in the Trinity.

She brings the road up to meet us,
allowing the sun's kiss to greet us
and the rain to fall softly on our face.

So I walk on the moonlight
intertwined with the sunlight
till all becomes one light.
Cats' eyes in the night.

The sum of expression between Creator and Son,
the Spirit casts words into the world,
but a poet is needed to set them free

and, at least for today, that's me.
My heartbeat drums love.

Part of creation's breath, Spellsong poetry
defeats mortality by shaping reality.
As peace, joy and wonder persist
in "Come and Become" we find rest.

VII
Sisters

The Elder breathes fire into pain
The Second speaks the truth of her youth
The Youngest writes words to be heard.

A changed family fabulation
ignites new truths spoken.
Stories burn. There's no return.

The Youngest reconnects, creating weft from what's left.
The Second's eidetic memory becomes the strong warp thread.
The Elder redirects her need to protect, weaving forgiveness
instead.

Understanding the imperative of creating a new narrative
these three Graces of many faces
turn to face the Lord as one

Love has won.

VIII
Bonfires

It's New Year's Eve. And though the Covid years have past,
we still use summer's firepit to make a night of it.
We aren't out the entire time, just from nine or so onwards.
Staying warm by huddling together in blanketed forms
we mark the year's turning with our bonfire burning.

Have you noticed how, if you start flame gazing,
the blazing orangey blue starts consuming you?
As your breath mists smoke, all other sounds choke.

I know that charcoal feeds fire, but as I clutch my prayer box,
realise that I'm curious as to whether desire and wishes
turned to ashes can rise again. And what about pain?

Dated ten years ago with coloured foam letters
this little box is filled with my cares. It's given great comfort,
this gift from my daughter, as has the writing of paper prayers.
Putting them in and letting them go has helped me go with the
flow.
And tonight, once again, that's what I've chosen to do.

One by one I toss them in, and in my reckoning,
there's been an answer to most of them.
The paper flies from my hand,
words lost before they land.

Before casting I read, seeing patterns
in how I thought and behaved, and realise
'it's the 'poor mes' and 'brave mes'
burning today.

Apart from the crackling, all is still.
My will shifts in the silence.
It's not just about letting go.
its knowing when to say yes and no.

As the sparks of light fly, my dragon uncoils.
She's become shining scales of copperplate-silver
a Daguerreotype mirror scored by fire
showing me now because I'm ready for how.

I have a right to be treated with respect,
to be circumspect when I say yes
and feel no guilt when it's the opposite.

To express myself and take time for myself
and have no regrets when I change my mind,
there are other ways to be kind.

It's better to be wrong than fake
and to have my cake and eat it,
beating others to it because my soul needs it.

Working hard can be good,
but not just because I should, stopping is fine too.
There are others who can do what I do.

If I'm defeated, I have the right to get up.
There's no need to soothe the victor's feelings,
my own have meaning.

Finally, I claim dignity and self-respect.
Without the need to direct everything
and protect everyone life can be fun.

As the flames start dying back,
I realise it's the crack of dawn
and think back to other long nights
when I let mistakes eat me and failure beat me.
I wish in my core I'd known this before,
given it space in a younger body, but I wasn't ready.

IX
The Candle And The Phoenix

"I want to be a candle," she says.
"Nicely scented, fragrance drifting.
Shifting haze lightly warming.
A pleasant, unobtrusive me.
Shining peaceably. "

"But you're not,' I say.
"You blaze and amaze.
Darkness dispelling; adversaries quelling –
Your courage puts fire enough in my belly
To proudly display, these...
My own feet of clay. "

"But I am a candle, " she says.
"Wick embedded in a jelly self
that wobbles a bit in its jar on the shelf.
The quivering flame not quite bright enough
to show up my wax-etched lack.
But the room smells nice.

"You can think you're a candle," I say.
But while you're busily filing the glass you sit in
in order to fit in
a phoenix arises.
Using the day's lassitude
it shapes fortitude.
Fanning the flame it calls your name.
Furious wings igniting the ashes from whence it came.
'Till you're the sum of all it's become."

"That's not true!" she cries.
"Stop veiling my eyes
with your dreams for me."

"Just be," I say.
"Let your tears fall, they heal the before.
You'll see beyond who you thought you were.
Fragments shattered, they lie scattered."

"And the scent burns as the world turns.
Winged Glory unfurled
You rise anew."

X
Knowing

Life is full of comings and goings: my boobs for one.
But, like any self-respecting crone, I still do glam.
I have make-up that glides over wrinkles,
and special pants hiding a stomach that crinkles
and droops – at the same time.

It's helpful to me that my eyes aren't as good
which means appearance is guided by mood.
From pyjama-clad cosy to 40+ glamorous
there is strength in my fuck-the-world fabulous.

I any case, I'm quite pleased with my face,
when I look in the mirror I'm still a disgrace.
Each drop of story in me is a mote in someone's eye,
as a pushing-past-perfectionist, insurgent insurrectionist
I know my worth. And will go to the ends of the earth
to call my soul my own.

Vibrant, courageous and beautiful
we crones can be dutiful
but we're dangerous too. Fearless.
In the face of happenstance we dance.

XI
Standing On Her Shoulders

I am walking. My cliff top eyrie path helps me chart the familiar
and the new.
Wild wind whipping at my hair, senses stripped bare, I am here
and I am there.
Looking down I see the white crested sea crashing against the
land.
The only bulwark is a strip of sand pebbled with seaweed-
headed chalk;
a mixture of chaos and order kissed into shape by the full-lipped
foam.

This twilight zone border pushes, displaces and replaces one
space with another;
a line of between, where water and land have been in an endless
tug of war,
a game of touch and withdraw played out for evermore. A swift
lover's kiss
then escape, but it's not clear who made the mistake each is
fleeing from.
I gaze at those waves, admiring the longevity of their brevity
and how
they've carved these landscape shapes; a presence here over
billions of years.

I hear them sing "Madeleine," inviting me in. Following their
summoning
I make my way down to the beach. I mark this jagged water-
wrought border,
a page torn from a book, with footprints in the sand. This is my
land.
I'm also forever pulled hither and hither, belonging to both and
neither,
chasing the exiled me. the maiden and mother I used to be
through time and space.

I rummage in my memories for those precious smells and tastes,
so different to this modern place. From the German forest's
earthy loam
to the streets of Leeds, my student home, to my Oma's house,
torn down.
I grieve for those childhood years and my simpler analogue life.
At least I've survived.
Though I'm trying to be brave, as I watch the waves tears salt
my face.

I follow time's inexorable will, modelled by the tide's turning,
feel myself burning to tell stories I've heard and kept inside.
I remember Nana telling me how her office was blown to bits in
the Blitz,
how she lived when others died. Eighty years gone, how the
world's moved on.

Her London no longer exists, nor does the one my mother knew,
nor the one
two of my children were born in. This brand-new century's
rooftop gardens
stretching as far as the Eye can see, were unknown to me then.

In a place only I can see, Nana and Oma are still part of me.
My imagination has created a world for the three of us and those
coming before and after us. Generations of our family stretching
out infinitely.

For now, though, my presence is demanded here. I've not yet
fully run my race,
patiently or at any other pace. So once again, I turn to the sea,
hoping it has answers for me.

Rocks fall from a green-fringed cliff's edge, a fuzzy divider
between me and the sky, where the gulls wheel by.
Life and death, as above, so below.
Separated by a single breath, one always following the other.
Despite that dividing line I feel my grandmothers' strength in
mine.

I think back to stories pulled from living memories. My great-
grandmother's wish for a ball,
and how her father's death meant her mother could barely
provide for the four of them.
It was only through self-reliance and strength she'd avoided the
workhouse door.
And my Oma's mother in Hitler's time handing out food parcels
bound by defiance
from a secret barn door and railing against the regime and all it
stood for.

As I get older, I hope someday stories will be told about me.
How I navigated chalk-circled rockpools
and man-made cesspools to be free,
wielding my pen as a sword to pass on stories.
I scream my own into the wind, for someone to find when they
can. I am.

We're all a collection of story stones. Each one built from the
bones of the other,
given life through the blood of our mothers, conjoined and
rejoined.

I'm a wind-whipped Medusa, a Confucius Storyteller, a Weaver.
I believe I can be a Life and Lightbringer as well as Death Singer.
As I've got older, I've got better at recognising the shoulders
I'm standing on.
I know who I am. So when they call "Come…"
I'll follow the other mothers, maidens and crones all the way
home.

XII
There Was Once A Writer

There was once a writer who was frightened of thoughts
so she swallowed them quickly before they were caught.

There was once a writer who wanted to flee
from the things she'd written for all to see.

There was once a writer who swallowed her words
How absurd to swallow your words!

She swallowed her words to prevent the escape
of other ideas she'd been trying to shape –
She was a fake.

There once was a writer who wanted to try
to jump off a cliff to discover the sky.

There once was a writer who understood
That resizing her ego would help her make good.

There once was a writer who knew it was true
that despite all the pain, writing's what she must do

So she continued to jump instead of swallowing
Her path determined, there was no time for wallowing

And her words were like birds
as they covered the sky –
She was free to fly.

EPILOGUE
THREADS

Love is red,
healing is blue,
poetry combines the two.

Cast fear aside and take up your thread...

ABOUT THE AUTHOR

Madeleine F White was born in Germany, with roots in Canada and the UK. Having produced a number of national and international web and print magazines, over the last few years she has focussed on being founder/editor of the Write On! suite of publications. As well as being published in a number of magazines and journals, Madeleine has also the authored the 2020 speculative debut novel *Mother Of Floods* and the related audio drama, *The Ark*, reached the top 50 in the Apple podcast charts.

ABOUT THE PRESS

Sea Crow Press is named for a flock of five talkative crows who live on a Cape Cod beach. According to Norse legend, one-eyed Odin sent two crows out into the world so they could return and tell its stories. If you sit and listen to the sea crows as they fly and roost and chatter, it's an easy legend to believe.

An award-winning woman-run independent publisher based in Massachusetts, Sea Crow Press is committed to amplifying voices that might otherwise go unheard. We publish creative nonfiction, literary fiction, and poetry. Our books celebrate our connection to each other and to the natural world with a focus on positive change and great storytelling.

ABOUT THE CROSSING PLACES SERIES

Maiden Mother Crone, the second book in *The Crossing Places Series*, is life affirming, nurturing and mothering. The series challenges women and our allies to come together to express experiences of the feminine through shared values, ideas and stories in different settings, particularly through nature and the natural world.

Though frame worked by the woman's narrative in *The Horse And The Girl* and the series' second book, *Maiden Mother Crone*, the third and forthcoming book, *The Maiden Mother Crone Anthology*, will give fathers, sons, brothers, partners and colleagues the opportunity to weave their voices and stories in alongside ours.

It is the intention of the Anthology to create space for the expression of feminine values; a shared dialogue that helps catalyse the world we want to build by putting care, empathy, and collaboration at the heart of everything we do.

If you'd like to find out more about The Crossing Places Series or wish to contribute to the anthology, please visit: seacrowpress.com/crossing-places-series

BV - #0086 - 110325 - C0 - 216/140/7 - PB - 9781961864245 - Matt Lamination